An Introduction to Coping with
Grief

2nd Edition

Sue Morris

ROBINSON

ROBINSON

First published in Great Britain in 2010 by Robinson
an imprint of Constable & Robinson Ltd

This edition published in 2017 by Robinson

1 3 5 7 9 10 8 6 4 2

A CIP catalogue record for this book
is available from the British Library.

Important note
This book is not intended as a substitute for medical advice
or treatment. Any person with a condition requiring medical
attention should consult a qualified medical practitioner
or suitable therapist.

ISBN: 978-1-47214-008-1

Typeset in Bembo by Initial Typesetting Services, Edinburgh
Printed and bound in Great Britain by CPI Group (UK) Ltd,
Croydon CR0 4YY.

Papers used by Robinson are from well-managed forests
and other responsible sources.

Robinson
An imprint of
Little, Brown Book Group
Carmelite House
50 Victoria Embankment
London EC4Y 0DZ

An Hachette UK Company
www.hachette.co.uk
www.littlebrown.co.uk

Contents

About This Book   vii

Part 1: About Grief   1

1 What Is Grief?   3

2 What to Expect When You're Grieving   11

3 The Reaction of Others   17

4 What Can Help?   21

Part 2: Coping with Grief   29

5 Tell Your Story   31

6 Establish a Routine   41

7 Carve Out Time to Grieve   49

8 Tackling Barriers   57

9 Dealing with 'Firsts'   73

10 Building Your New Path   79

Other Things that Might Help   95

About This Book

Grief is something that most of us will experience at some point in our lives. How we react when someone we love dies will be different for each of us because grief is unique. There's no right or wrong way to grieve. One of the hardest parts for people who are grieving is working out what they need to do to help themselves at a time when they feel especially vulnerable and alone.

You may be reading this book because you've lost someone very special in your life – maybe your partner, child, parent, sibling or close friend. Even though you know that there's nothing that anyone can do to bring them back, you can begin to do things that will help you feel a little more in control of your grief. This book, which is divided into two parts, will show you how. Part 1 describes the nature of grief and what you might experience. Part 2 describes a number of strategies or tools that you can use to help you take charge of your life again, while learning how to maintain a connection with your loved one.

As you read on, you will find information about grief and what to expect as well as a number of different exercises to help you adjust to the death of your loved one and the changes you're facing. It's recommended to read the book from beginning to end and then go back and review the sections that are most relevant to you. It's also a good idea to write down your answers in the spaces provided, which allows you to keep a record of your work and, at the same time, track your progress.

This book is designed for you to use on your own. If, however, you feel overwhelmed and think you're getting worse, talk to your family doctor about what other options might be available, especially as grief tends to be far more stressful than most people think. Counselling from a qualified grief specialist or attending a support group can be of great benefit. It's important, however, to remember that there's no magic cure. Unfortunately, grief cannot be hurried, as it tends to have a life of its own. It's important to be patient with yourself because dealing with grief can be both exhausting and overwhelming.

Take care,
Sue Morris

Part 1: ABOUT GRIEF

1

What is Grief?

Grief can be described as the intense emotional and physical reaction that someone experiences following the death of a loved one. Grief is not only characterised by deep sadness but also by an intense longing or yearning to be with that person again. Even though grief can be particularly painful, it is a normal reaction to loss and, in time, most people learn to adjust to life without their loved one. In psychological terms, grief is defined[*] as the anguish experienced after significant loss, usually the death of a beloved person, and this is the focus of this book. However, people can also experience grief associated with other losses, such as divorce, retirement or after being diagnosed with a serious illness.

[*] Definition from *APA Dictionary of Psychology* by G. R. VandenBos (ed.), published by the American Psychological Association (2007).

Emotional and physical reactions

The death of a loved one is believed to be the most powerful stressor in everyday life. When someone you love dies, your life changes forever from the moment you learn about their death. In the early weeks and months, you're likely to experience a number of intense emotional and physical reactions even if the death was expected. You may at times think you're going crazy or you may feel completely numb. If you've recently lost someone you love, you're likely to have experienced one or more of the following:

Some common physical reactions

- crying

- feeling sick

- feeling numb

- headaches

- muscle tension

- racing heart

- difficulty sleeping

- not feeling like eating

- fear

- panic

- stomach upset

- agitation or restlessness

- aches and pains

Some common emotional reactions

- yearning or pining

- intense sadness

- shock

- disbelief

- despair

- worry

- guilt

- anger

- emptiness

- peace

- relief

- confusion

Even though these feelings can be very distressing and you want them to stop, it's important to remind yourself that grief is a normal response when some-one you loved has died and, in time, these feelings will lessen.

Grief is complex

Grief is far more complex than most people expect because it's made up of three important compo-nents that each need to be addressed: loss, change and control.

Loss

When someone dies, we naturally focus on 'who' died. But with any death comes the loss of so many other things. In losing this person, you may also lose your best friend, your companion, your lover, your accountant or the person you relied on most for support. If you've lost someone who was ill for a long time and you were their main carer, you may also miss the contact you had with the health professionals who were involved in their treatment and the daily routine you followed.

Being able to identify what you've lost is an import-ant first step because it relates to the complexity of your grief. Not only are you grieving the loss of the person, but you're grieving the loss of the life you had with them and your hopes and dreams for your future. Even though grieving can at times be very painful, in fact it's good because it gives you the time and space to adjust to life without your loved one.

Change

The many different losses that you are likely to experience result in varying degrees of change. How much your life changes after the death often matches the extent your lives overlapped, both emotionally and physically. Being able to adjust to these many changes takes time and effort because it requires you to try new things. You may also find it harder to think clearly and to concentrate, which is why you need to be patient with yourself and take things slowly. If, however, you find yourself thinking about suicide or not being here any more, then seek help immediately from your family doctor, hospital, or local crisis line such as the Samaritans.

Tip

Be patient – remind yourself that grief is made up of loss and change, which involves new learning and a period of adjustment.

Kate's story

'My husband Craig died six weeks ago. He had been diagnosed in the summer with bowel cancer. The doctors at first seemed optimistic about his treatment and we never entertained the idea that he wouldn't make it. In fact, we never actually talked about him dying, even though that now sounds strange. I really wish we had because he would have been able to tell me what to do. I'm worried about whether I'll have to move and wonder how I'll manage financially. We have an old house that Craig was fixing up and now everything seems to be going wrong with it. I've gone back to my job but I don't know how I'll pay all the bills. I'm sure my friends are getting sick of me by now but I just feel so alone. I miss him so much. I wish he hadn't left me in this mess. I don't know what I am going to do or where my life is heading.'

Control

Control is another important aspect of grief. When somebody you love dies, you have little or no control over the circumstances surrounding their death. You might feel overwhelmed by your grief as though it has total control over you. You may wonder how you will get everything done, or ask yourself whether or not you'll ever feel like your old self again. Part of coping with grief is learning how to begin taking control over your grief rather than letting it consume you. You'll see how to do this in Part 2.

'When my four-month-old daughter died from Sudden Infant Death Syndrome (SIDS), my life as I knew it was totally shattered. I quickly learned that having control over one's life was an illusion.'

Sienna, thirty-three years

2

What to Expect When You're Grieving

If your grief is new, you may experience some of the following thoughts and feelings:

- feeling overwhelmed

- difficulty concentrating

- lethargy or tiredness

- feeling fuzzy in the head

- thinking that you're going crazy or losing your mind

- pining or yearning for the person who has died

- having little motivation

- experiencing difficulty learning or taking in new information

- difficulty in making decisions

- being unable to control your emotions

- feeling less tolerant of others

- crying easily

- wanting to be alone

- not wanting to be alone

- feeling fearful or anxious

- having dreams or nightmares about death and dying

- dreaming about your loved one

- entertaining thoughts of dying so that you can be with them.

Grief is unique

Almost everybody who is grieving asks, 'How long will I feel this way?' Unfortunately, when you're grieving it's impossible to know how long your pain will last. In fact, no two people will experience the death of someone close to them in the same way. How you grieve will depend on many factors including:

- your personality

- the way you tend to deal with problems

- the type of relationship you had with the person who died

- the way you think about things that happen to you in your life

- the circumstances surrounding the death.

Expectations

Having a sense of what to expect when you're grieving will help you get through each day a little better. Today we live in a fast-paced and technology-driven world with a 'fix it', 'can do' mentality. We want things done immediately and we tend to have little patience with ourselves and others. We send an email or a text and expect an instant reply, or when we're sick we go to the doctor and expect a prescription to make us feel better. Unfortunately, grief doesn't follow these same rules. It knows no timetables and it can't be hurried. Grief is not an illness, nor is it something that you can just 'get over' and 'get back to normal'. It's different for everyone and will involve many ups and downs.

The wave-like pattern of grief

It's helpful to think of grief as coming in waves, where over time the intensity and frequency of the waves lessen. Many people say that the waves of grief come often and are very strong soon after the death of a loved one. As time passes, the strength of the waves decreases. Other people find that their waves of grief may not peak in intensity until several months after the death, when the reality and finality of the death sink in. 'Trigger waves', which are usually accompanied by intense emotions, can occur at any time and often seem as though they come out of the blue. They can include anything from seeing someone who looks like the person who has died to hearing a song on the radio. They can also coincide with significant dates such as birthdays or anniversaries. What tends to happen is that the trigger wave peaks, then the wave-like pattern continues on. It's important to realise that trigger waves are normal and not a sign that you're getting worse.

If you expect that grief will follow a wave-like pattern then you won't be surprised when you have a 'bad' day after thinking you were coping quite well. In time your waves of grief will lessen in intensity and frequency, and things will get easier. It's helpful to expect that you will have a mixture of good and bad days for at least the first year or so, rather than think you will be 'back to normal' within months. Hopefully, as the first year goes on, you will have more good days than bad days and in the second year, more good days again. Healthy grieving involves getting through all the firsts: birthdays, holidays, significant dates and the first anniversary of their death. Remember that there's no magic cure for grief – there's no quick fix.

For some, the second year might seem harder as the reality of the loss sets in. This can be true for those whose loved one died suddenly or 'out of order', as with the death of a child or a young adult who had their lives ahead of them. It's normal in situations like this to expect that your wave of grief might follow a longer trajectory, which is why it is important to seek support so that you aren't doing this alone.

Tip

Remember that grief follows a wave-like pattern, which will be different for everyone.

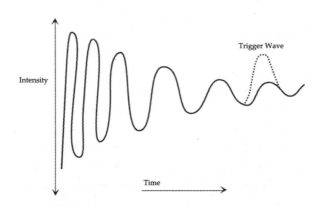

Anna's story

'My mother died suddenly when my first baby was three months old. I don't think the full impact of her death hit me until the first anniversary. Up until that time, even though I was sad and missed her terribly, my life was consumed with taking care of my daughter. I found counselling helped me understand why I was feeling worse one year on. Thinking about my grief in terms of a wave really made sense to me.'

3

The Reaction of Others

When you're grieving you're likely to be given lots
of advice by well-meaning friends and family. Some
of this advice may be really helpful and some may
make you feel worse. Unhelpful comments about
grief tend to stem from the belief in our society that
showing strong emotions such as sadness is a sign
of weakness. We also tend to believe that we can
'fix' all of our problems. Unfortunately, death is a
problem we can't fix.

If your loved one has recently died, you may hear
the following or think these things yourself:

- You've got to get on with your life.

- You've got to get over it.

- You've got to pull yourself together.

- You've got to think of the children.

- You've got to stop crying.

- You should be better by now.

- You've got to be thankful that they had a 'good' life.

These types of comments are usually attempts to solve your sadness; to make you feel better even though they can often have the opposite effect. When someone says 'you've got to get over it', or you think it to yourself, what they are really trying to do is to offer a solution to take away your pain – to 'fix' you. Unfortunately, there are no words to stop your pain. What would be more helpful is if we give ourselves and other people permission to grieve by acknowledging their pain and allowing them the necessary time and space to adjust to life without the person who has died. To do this requires that we hold realistic beliefs about grief and how those who are bereaved should behave.

Realistic beliefs include:

- Grief is unique.

- There's no quick fix for grief.

- Grief isn't over in an instant.

- Grief is a normal response to loss.

- Grieving is healthy as it gives you the time to adjust to life without that person.

- Crying is one way to express grief.

- Grief is not the same as depression.

- It's normal to feel very sad when someone you love dies.

- If you loved deeply, you can't expect to grieve shallowly.

- Grief is not an illness with a prescribed cure.

- Grief follows a wave-like pattern that will be different for everyone.

- Until you've reached the first anniversary of the death, many of the triggers to your grief remain unknown.

- Children benefit from learning that grief is a normal reaction to loss.

If those around you are impatient for you to get 'back to normal', you may need to speak up for yourself and remind others that there's no quick fix because death is not a problem that can be solved. Rather grieving is the process that allows you slowly to 'get used' to your life without your loved one.

Tip

Remember, grief is not an illness with a cure; it is a normal response to loss.

4

What Can Help?

Grief can be a very lonely and isolating experience. One of the hardest things about grieving is that no one else can do it for you. At times you may wonder whether what you're experiencing is 'normal'. You may have lots of questions and few answers. You may also have many well-intentioned friends who tell you that they know how you're feeling and what you should be doing. But because grieving is something that you need to do for yourself, the best advice is to take things slowly, one step at a time, and listen to your grief – don't fight it. You may have been told that time heals all wounds. While there is an element of truth in this statement, what really makes the difference is what you do in the time. Working out what you need to do to help yourself adjust to your loved one's death is crucial.

People who are grieving need to be able to:

- tell their story about their loved one's death

- give themselves permission to grieve

- find ways to regain a sense of control

- build a different path without that person in their life.

Wound analogy

Most people believe that grief needs to be expressed even though it hurts. The 'wound analogy' is helpful in understanding why it's so important to express your grief in some way.

Imagine you have a huge, infected wound on your leg that's causing you severe pain. It's deep and raw. Before it can begin to heal over you need to get the infection out. You may need antibiotic treatment or a daily dressing. Only after the infection has gone will the wound start to heal properly. Over time, the wound will become less tender and eventually you'll be able to touch it without causing pain. But a scar will always remain and you'll be able to recall the pain that was associated with how you got the wound in the first place.

Even though this is a crude analogy, it demonstrates the need for you to express your grief if it's causing you distress. There are many different ways to do this, which will be described in Part 2. In the long run, it won't help if you put on a brave front and hide your emotions. In fact it's likely to make it worse. Having said that, it's important to realise that some of you will not have the same need to talk about the death, especially if you're a very private person and want to keep it to yourself. Neither way is better than the other because grief is unique. It's up to you to work out what is best for you.

Medication

Many people ask whether medication such as anti-depressants will help them when they are grieving. This is an understandable question because they want their pain to stop. As a general rule, anti-depressant medication is not routinely recommended for grief because grief is considered a normal response to loss and is not the same as depression, even though at times it may seem unbearable. It is, however, a question that you should ask your family doctor because everyone's circumstances are different. If you have a history of depression or other mental illness, for example, then your doctor will be able to help work out what is best for you.

Sometimes people are prescribed anti-anxiety medication or sleeping tablets for a short period of time following the death. It's important to avoid becoming dependent on such medications and to use them with caution. Consult your doctor because none of these can take away the pain of losing your loved one.

Tip

Let your family doctor know about the death of your loved one so that they can make recommendations about your care as needed.

Counselling

Counselling is an option to consider if you think you would benefit from speaking to someone apart from your immediate family and friends. While many people don't seek counselling, it can be extremely beneficial, especially for those who don't have a strong support network in their local community or in cases where the death was traumatic or unexpected, such as after an accident or suicide. Even though you may feel really sad talking about the death, most people feel better for being able to do so in a safe environment where they can freely express their thoughts and feelings without being told how they should feel or what they should do. If you think you'd like to try it, ask your family doctor or local hospice for a referral to someone who is experienced in grief counselling.

Tip

Seek help immediately from your family doctor or local hospital if you feel suicidal or hopeless about your future.

Support groups

Even though you may have never participated in a group before or if you do not consider yourself to be a 'group person', bereavement support groups can help you feel less isolated and alone. They provide a forum where you can meet others who have experienced a similar loss while also learning strategies to cope with the many changes that you may be facing as a result of your loss. Most hospice programmes offer support groups that are open to the community as well as many faith-based organisations.

James's story

'When my wife died at twenty-nine years of age from breast cancer, I felt as though my whole world as I knew it stopped. I was devastated and didn't know how to go on. None of my friends and family knew how to help me – I felt so alone. The hospital social worker who had cared for my wife suggested I join a support group for younger adults whose partners had also died. I was unsure at first as I'd never been to a group before but I went because I didn't know what else to do. Now nearly a year later, I can say that the group has been the best thing for me as I've met other people who can relate to how I am feeling – they just get it.'

This book is based on the psychological therapy known as cognitive behaviour therapy (CBT), which is a widely used form of therapy that focuses on the link between thinking, feelings and behaviour. CBT works very well when dealing with the death of someone close to you because it helps you identify and tackle unhelpful thoughts that may be keeping you stuck. It also helps you try new things even if you're understandably reluctant to do so. In Part 2 you will find a number of exercises and strategies based on CBT that will help you learn to take control of your grief.

Part 2: COPING WITH GRIEF

5

Tell Your Story

Each of you will have a different story to tell about how your loved one died and the impact it has had on your life. Regardless of whether the death was expected or sudden, being able to tell your story in some way will help you make sense of what has happened.

Even if you don't like talking about personal things, it's still important to ask yourself whether or not you've had the opportunity to talk about their death. Some people won't feel the need to talk at all and prefer to think through things on their own, whereas others need to talk to express their thoughts and feelings. Sometimes they need to tell their story over and over. If you're someone who wants to talk about your loved one, often the hardest part is finding someone you trust who can truly listen to you. Often as time goes on, it's common to talk less for fear of burdening others. It will be important to find a few special people who are prepared to keep listening to you as you attempt to navigate the changes you face. Sometimes speaking to a grief counsellor or attending a support group can help.

When you're thinking about your story, the following questions may help you:

- Who died?

- How did they die?

- Was their death expected or unexpected?

- What have you lost with the death of this person?

- What thoughts or feelings are worrying you?

- Who can support you as you grieve?

- What would your loved one want for you now?

- Which direction do you see your life taking now?

Let's look at Alice's story:

Alice's story

'My husband Tom was sixty years old when he was diagnosed with a brain tumour. He seemed fit and healthy until a few weeks before the doctors gave us the horrible news.

He then went downhill very quickly and it all seems a blur. We'd been married for thirty-six years and have three children. About ten years ago I nearly left our marriage because I found out that Tom was having an affair. It was a very tough few years together but we both worked hard to save our marriage. It seemed that we had finally got our lives back on track and that it was now our time as our children had left home. We were planning our retirement together doing all the things that we hadn't had the time or money to do when the kids were younger. I saw it very much as our "second chance". I am now so sad and also angry about what has happened. I feel really cheated. I have so many questions – why did this happen to us? Why couldn't the doctors save him? It's just not fair and I feel all alone. My children just want me to "get over it" and I can't really talk to them as they never knew about the affair. My doctor suggested I see a counsellor.'

When Alice went to see a counsellor, it was really important that she could first of all tell her story – not just the story of her husband's death, but the story of their life together – their history, both good and the bad, as well as their hopes for the future. Let's look at how Alice answered her counsellor's questions about her story.

Alice's session

Who died?

Husband, Tom.

How did they die?

Brain tumour.

Was their death expected or unexpected?

Unexpected – it happened very quickly.

What you have you lost with the death of your loved one?

Partner, travelling companion, my handyman, my second chance at a very happy marriage; our retirement.

Who can support you as you grieve?

Our children can to some degree. I also have a few close friends who know about the affair and are great at inviting me out but they still have their husbands so they really don't know what I am going through. My doctor is supportive and now I am attending counselling.

What would your loved one want for you now?

Tom would want me to continue to plan my retirement and travel to the places we had talked about visiting. He wouldn't want me to be this sad. I think he would also say – as he often did – that we did get our life back on track and we were stronger for it as a couple. He would want me to remind myself of this.

Which direction do you see your life taking now?

I'm not sure. I will have to think about what I can do. I will have to think about what I can do without him. I don't have to sell the house, which is good. Luckily, I have my health. I would like to travel, so I will need to find out about different options. I would also like to spend more time with my grandchildren.

Alice was able to begin to make sense of what she was experiencing by telling her story. With her counsellor, she was also able to talk freely about the difficult time in her marriage without feeling that she was betraying her husband's memory. Answering these questions gave her an opportunity to acknowledge the different aspects of her grief and think about what she needed to do to help gain more control of it. Try answering these questions for yourself in the space beneath – remember there are no right or wrong answers.

Tip

Being able to tell your story will help you make sense of what has happened.

Exercise: Tell your story

Who died?

_____

_____

How did they die?

_____

_____

_____

_____

_____

Who can support you as you grieve?

_____

_____

_____

_____

_____

Was their death expected or unexpected?

_____

_____

_____

_____

_____

What have you lost with the death of your loved one?

_____

_____

_____

_____

What thoughts or feelings are worrying you?

_____

_____

_____

_____

What would your loved one want for you now?

_____

_____

_____

_____

Which direction do you see your life taking now?

_____

_____

_____

_____

Peter's story

'My sixteen-year-old son died after a two-year battle with bone cancer. A year or so after his death, I was invited to join the patient and family advisory committee at the hospital where he was treated. Being a part of this group has helped me tremendously as I am able to talk about my son while also helping others. It keeps me connected to him and that time in our life.'

6

Establish a Routine

If you're reading this book soon after your loved one has died, it's important to establish a daily routine straight away, no matter how simple. It may be having a shower and eating a light breakfast as soon as you get out of bed each morning. Or it may be driving to the shops to buy the newspaper or taking the dog for a walk. A routine helps because you don't need to think about what to do next and it will allow you to save your energy for other things. Eating well and being physically active are important too because people who are grieving are more prone to develop health problems caused by the stress that they are under, both physically and emotionally. Make sure you limit how much alcohol you drink because alcohol is a depressant and can interfere with your mood and sleep.

The following tips might help you think about your well-being and how to go about establishing a routine.

- Plan to eat at regular meal times.

- Try to eat something even if you don't feel like it.

- Avoid processed foods.

- Limit your alcohol intake.

- Prepare extra quantities of food to freeze.

- Invite a friend over to eat with you.

- Walk wherever you can.

- Try to build some form of activity into your day.

- Remind yourself that sleeping difficulties are a normal reaction following the death of someone close to you and they are usually temporary.

- Write a daily 'to do' list and tick off each item as you do it.

- Create folders or files for the paperwork that needs to be completed.

- Set aside a defined period of time in your week to attend to business matters.

- Contact your HR department at work – see what your options are about taking leave and returning to work.

- Visit your family doctor for a check-up; keep them informed of what has happened.

- Seek counselling if you feel overwhelmed or have little support.

Part of your daily routine can also include the business matters that need to be finalised if you are the next of kin or involved in the estate. Many people find dealing with these matters overwhelming and they can be a constant source of worry. Learning how to compartmentalise or separate your worries is a useful strategy.

Compartmentalising your worries

Imagine that you have a number of different boxes that you can fill with your worries. Each box has a lid that you can use to close the box to contain your worries. The 'worry boxes' exercise helps you prioritise what you need to do, while at the same time it helps you increase your sense of control.

Exercise: Worry boxes

Step 1 Make a list of the issues that are worrying you right now.

Step 2 Group these issues into different categories.

Step 3 Write a label that defines each of these groups you made in Step 2. For example: finances, house, car, children, work and so on.

Step 4 Now imagine that you can take each group of issues and store them in a box. Each box has a lid that you can close.

Step 5 Within each box or category, sort the issues in order of priority. What needs to be done right now? What can wait? Put an asterisk next to the items that you want to address first.

Step 6 What action can you now take to address the issues you marked with an asterisk?

Remember Kate from Part 1? Let's look at how she categorised and prioritised her worries.

Kate's priorities

Finances/legal issues

General finances

Changing bank account details★

Paying the mortgage

Finalising the will★

Kate – personal

Feeling alone★

Not being able to stop crying★

Feel like I'm burdening friends★

Regretting not discussing Craig's death★

Craig's things

Sorting through Craig's belongings

Selling Craig's car

Disconnecting his mobile phone★

House

Upkeep of old house

Leaking toilet★

Replying to sympathy cards★

Kate – work

Finding a better-paid job

Even though Kate still had many big decisions to make, she felt less overwhelmed after she had organised her worries in this way. She realised she didn't need to do everything straight away. Based on the items that she placed an asterisk next to, Kate was able to work out her next steps and make a 'to-do' list:

- Make an appointment to see bank manager.

- Make an appointment to see lawyer about the will.

- Call the plumber.

- Reply to two sympathy cards each day.

- Contact the mobile phone company.

- See doctor for a check-up and referral to grief counsellor to talk about Craig's death and her regrets.

Making a daily 'to-do' list will help you feel as though you're taking control and provide a structure for your day. Use a diary or calendar to write down what needs to be done by when. Prioritise and be patient with yourself about what you can achieve each day. Remember, when you're grieving you might have difficulty concentrating or taking information in, so aim to do a few things each day and tick them off once you've done them. Ask for help and delegate where you can.

If you have lots of paperwork to do, develop a filing system. Use different colour folders to represent the different categories listed in the worry box exercise. That way you can file the paperwork as you receive it and keep it together in one place until it needs to be dealt with. For example, you might have different colour folders for finances, house bills and the car. Having a real box with a lid is also a good idea to store your loved one's keepsakes. You then have all the items in one place if at a later date you choose to make a memory book or album.

Sorting through things in this way helps you to maintain some order and increases your sense of control.

Tip

Use different colour folders to organise your paperwork.

Even though you may not feel like doing anything after your loved one has died, a general rule of thumb is that having things to do and commitments to keep will help you get through each day a little more easily. The aim is to take small steps in the beginning – a day or even an hour at a time. Being distracted by a task for a few moments each day can help you get through those early months. Don't wait to 'feel' like doing something; just do it.

7

Carve Out Time to Grieve

There are no specific guidelines or rules about how to express your grief, but most people say that they feel better when they let their grief out in some way. There are many ways to do this such as crying, talking, exercising, listening to music, attending a support group, seeing a counsellor, writing about your grief and being creative. Being able to tell your story is not only for people who had wonderful relationships. Coming to terms with difficult relationships is also a part of grieving. Perhaps your relationship with the person who died was full of heartache; maybe you felt you were constantly let down; maybe you were waiting for things to get better. Whatever your relationship was, grief is better out than in. And in letting it out, it's important to set aside time to grieve. Even though this may be very hard to do because it's painful, be patient and remind yourself that 'sad isn't bad' when you're dealing with the death of someone close to you.

Heather's story

'My mother and I had always had a rocky relationship. I never felt that she really loved me or that I could ever please her. When I got married, I saw her less often as she made it clear she didn't approve of my husband. Her death has bothered me more than I thought it would. I tried hard not to think about it but it was always there in the back of my mind.

Through counselling I realised that I was really grieving the loss of the mother–daughter relationship that I had always wanted and hoped for. Talking about it to someone impartial has been really positive as it made me acknowledge that, even though our relationship was tough, I still loved her and her me in her own strange way.'

Set aside time to grieve

Like any important task, it's important to 'carve out' time to grieve by scheduling it into your day. If you don't make time, it's easy to become consumed with the busyness of life and you risk pushing your grief aside. People with young children or hectic careers, for example, can find themselves in this situation. It's not intentional – it just happens.

Planning a specific time each day or every couple of days to sit down and think about the death of your loved one helps you to feel more in control of your grief. One suggestion is to allocate twenty to thirty minutes each or every other day as your 'grief time'. Choose a time when you won't be interrupted and don't have to rush off immediately afterwards. Use a journal to write down your thoughts and feelings and date your entries, so you can look back over your journal and track your progress.

The following list gives you some ideas about what to do in your 'grief time':

- Sit quietly, close your eyes and think about the person who has died.

- Play music that reminds you of them.

- Talk to them about your day as though they were sitting next to you.

- Allow yourself to cry – remember that sad isn't bad.

- Write in your journal.

- Write your loved one a letter.

- List the things you miss about them.

- Write about the events as you know them surrounding their death.

- List any questions you may want answered.

- Look through photographs of your time together.

- Make a 'to-do' list about what needs to be done.

- Do something creative such as painting or gardening.

- Make a memory book that tells their story – include photos, cards and other mementos.

- Use email to ask your loved one's friends to contribute memories of how they met, funny stories and what they valued most about them.

- Spend time outdoors.

- Read self-help books or join an online support group.

By scheduling time in this way, you're compartmentalising or containing your grief. Although it may be painful to focus on your grief, many people say that they actually feel 'better' when they do set time aside on a regular basis, because they feel more able to get on with the rest of their day. In time, you probably won't feel the need to carve out as much time to grieve and may write less often in your journal.

Writing to your loved one

Many people find writing to their loved one on a regular basis very helpful. It can be a wonderful way to express your grief, and at the same time it helps you maintain a connection with them. You can write as a part of your 'grief time' or you can write whenever you feel the need. There's no right or wrong way to do this. One useful guideline is to write things down that you would ordinarily say to them. The advantage of writing down your thoughts and feelings is that it takes more brain power to put your thoughts down on paper than just thinking them through. Writing can also be a great way to try to make sense of things that may be troubling you.

Here are some suggestions about ways to start:

- It's been _____ days/weeks/months since you've been gone and I wanted to tell you ___
  _____.

- If you were here right now, I would tell you/ ask you _____.

- Before you died I wish I'd had the chance to tell you _____. I am not sure what to do about _____
  _____ and wondered what your advice would be?

- I wanted to tell you about how I've been getting on and the changes that have happened to me since you died _____
  _____
  _____
  _____
  _____.

Let's look at John's story.

John's story

'When my son died in a car accident I just couldn't talk to anyone about him. If I did I'd just get all choked up, which seemed to embarrass everyone, not just me. He had left several months before his death to start university and we hadn't seen each other for three months. He was really happy and making friends. My wife and I had planned to visit him the week before he died and we were going to spend some time fishing, which is something we loved to do together. But we put the trip off thinking we'd go in a few more weeks when the weather warmed up. I feel so guilty – why didn't we go when we planned? If only we'd gone – something might have changed and he might not have been in the car at the time of the accident. I can't stop thinking about him and how he died. I'm drinking too much and finding it hard to get out of bed each day. Our younger kids are struggling too. I don't think I am being a very good father or husband but I just don't know what to do.'

John wasn't a talker but he did need to find a way to express his grief about his son. Even though it was very difficult, John planned a special fishing trip on his own back to their favourite fishing spot. He then set aside some time each evening in the weeks before to write his son the following letter. He chose to read the letter out loud around the camp fire and burn it afterwards. While this didn't take away John's pain, he did feel that he had taken an important step forward in tackling his grief, which allowed him to focus more on the rest of his family and his own health. John decided that he would regularly return to their fishing spot, often taking his other children. In doing so, he created a new tradition that allowed him to remain connected to his son.

Hey kiddo,

It's been nearly two months since you've been gone and I wanted to tell you how much I really miss you. I can't believe you aren't here any more. It's not the way it's meant to be. Your old man should be the one to go first. Your mum is really sad and Hannah and Josh are so quiet – they really miss their big brother. But today I've decided to go fishing at Sanden river – just like the good old times. We loved this place and it holds so many good memories. I think you were about three when I first took you here to fish. Just the boys. I know you would want us to get on with things but it's just so hard. But I will try. I will be back in a few weeks and let you know how I am doing then.

Dad

8

Tackling Barriers

Barriers to dealing with grief can include:

- unanswered questions

- distressing feelings

- avoiding certain places or people that remind you of your loved one

- having difficulty making decisions.

As with any barrier, if you want to move forward you need to be able to get past it in some way. In grief, the barriers can be very painful, so often people try not to think about them, hoping that they will go away. Unfortunately, it doesn't work like this. Often the barriers become even greater over time, and harder to tackle.

Worrying thoughts and feelings

Is there anything concerning the death of your loved one that's playing over and over in your mind? Common barriers to dealing with grief can include unanswered questions, asking, 'Why?', wishing you'd said or done something differently, and feelings of guilt, anger or regret. Thinking that life should be fair can also become a potential barrier. If you do have a strong belief that we live in a fair and just world, this belief will be challenged when someone you love dies prematurely, especially if their death was unexpected. Being able to change the way you think will help you overcome your barriers. You will see how to do this in the exercise 'Unanswered questions'.

Unanswered questions

If you have unanswered questions surrounding the death of your loved one, your brain is likely to go over and over possible explanations, in an attempt to try to make sense of the facts as you know them. Not knowing why or how someone died is a huge barrier to coming to terms with it. Often there are no simple answers. If you do have questions, you may feel better if you try to find answers by speaking to people who were involved, such as health professionals, witnesses or the police. In the case of suicide, trying to understand the events that led to the death could help. Did they leave a note? Were they behaving differently beforehand? Were they getting help? You might also benefit from discussing your questions with a grief counsellor who can help you explore the possible answers. It's also important to accept that you may never know or understand fully what happened.

Exercise: Unanswered questions

- Write down any questions you have about their death.

- Is there any literature that might help you understand the situation more fully?

- Who could you contact to answer these questions?

- Make an appointment with them and explain why you're coming so they can prepare.

Once you have this information, write down the possible answers to your questions that make the most sense to you.

Asking 'Why?'

Similarly, trying to answer this question is another important part of attempting to accept your loved one's death and it will likely take time. If the death was unexpected you may well be struggling with the question 'Why?', because it wasn't meant to be that way. How you expected life to be is not how it has turned out. Being able to express your heartache over and over can help. Some people find that the death of someone close raises lots of spiritual or religious questions and find it helps to speak to someone from their faith group.

Janet's story

'When my husband Steve died by suicide, I didn't know why. There were so many unanswered questions. He had suffered from depression for many years but had just started treatment with a new psychiatrist and all seemed to be going well. Even though it was something that had always been in the back of my mind, he was much happier within himself than he had been for a long time. One thing that helped me was that I met with his psychiatrist soon after his death as I wanted to understand more about how he seemed when he last saw him. At the time, my family doctor also recommended a support group for survivors of suicide because it was hard to be with our friends, as they didn't know what to say. I found that it was good to be able to talk to people who had experienced the same type of loss.'

Guilt, anger or regret

If you're struggling with a strong sense of guilt, anger or regret, then these feelings can also become barriers to dealing with your grief and need to be addressed. Identifying the thoughts or beliefs that lead to these emotions is an important first step. Let's look at them separately.

Guilt is the emotion people experience when they think they have done something wrong, whether or not they actually have. If the thoughts leading to feelings of guilt are left unchallenged, it can become a very destructive emotion.

Anger can also be a huge barrier to many people as it keeps them stuck and unable to move forward.

Regret is an emotion that many people express at some level. Regret about things not said, regret about things never done, and regret about hopes for the future. Sometimes people have regret over the medical decisions that were made, especially if their loved one had been ill for a while.

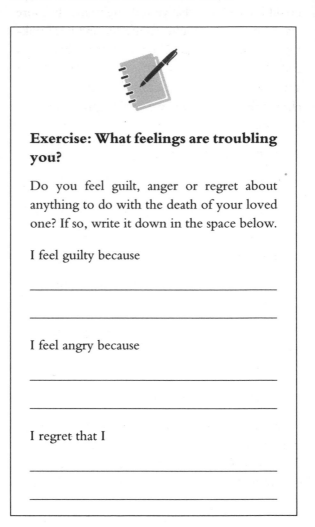

Exercise: What feelings are troubling you?

Do you feel guilt, anger or regret about anything to do with the death of your loved one? If so, write it down in the space below.

I feel guilty because

_____

_____

I feel angry because

_____

_____

I regret that I

_____

_____

In all parts of our life, the way we think about things affects how we feel and behave. Grieving is no different except that your thoughts may be more distorted because you're vulnerable and not thinking as clearly as usual. The thoughts we have on a daily basis – known as 'self-talk' – tend to occur automatically and affect our mood. If we want to change the way we feel, we need to change the way we think.

To do this, ask yourself the following questions:

1. Where's the evidence for what I think?

2. What are the alternatives to what I think?

3. What is the likely effect on me of thinking in this way?

4. How would I advise a friend to think in the same situation?

5. What would my loved one say if they were here now?

Let's look at an example.

Peggy, Jack's wife of forty-four years, was dying from pancreatic cancer. She had deteriorated suddenly and was in a lot of pain. They had hoped she would be able to die at home under the care of their local hospice. In the final few days, Jack didn't think he could care properly for Peggy at home and she was admitted to hospital where she later died. When Jack completed the above exercise he wrote:

> *I feel guilty because I let Peggy down by not being able to care for her at home until she died.*

Using questions one, two and five, Jack began to challenge his thinking. He was eventually able to tell himself this:

> *There's no evidence that I failed Peggy. I tried my best to keep her at home but her disease got the better of us in the end. I wish things could have been different, but I know I did all I could. Peggy would say that going to the hospital was the best decision given the circumstances and limited choices we had.*

Avoiding people or places

If you've been avoiding a certain person or place since your loved one died, you need to decide how to tackle your avoidance because it will only make things harder in the end. Often people avoid certain rooms in their house, favourite restaurants, visiting the grave or talking to others about the death. You may be worried that you won't be able to stop crying and so avoid putting yourself in certain situations. But there's a fine line between not being ready to face something that's difficult and avoiding it. Unfortunately, the problem with avoidance is that while it may help ease your pain in the beginning, it will only make your grief worse in the long run.

The following exercise will help you work out a plan to approach what or who you're avoiding. If, however, you don't think you can do it on your own, you might benefit from seeing a grief counsellor who can help you examine your thinking and face the situations you're avoiding in a gradual way. Below is how Janet answered these questions soon after her husband Steve died by suicide. She and her husband had been one of four close couples who went out on a regular basis.

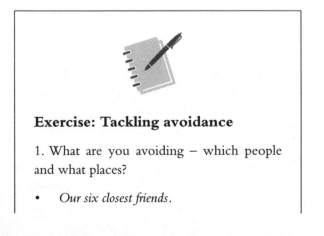

Exercise: Tackling avoidance

1. What are you avoiding – which people and what places?

* *Our six closest friends.*

2. Develop a hierachy of items, from easiest to hardest, to help tackle what you are avoiding.

- *Seeing the three women at my house first.*
- *Inviting their husbands with them to my house.*
- *The seven of us going out together to a local restaurant.*

3. For each item, write down what you fear about the item you're avoiding.

- *I fear that I will start crying and not be able to stop.*
- *I fear that if I cry the men will be uncomfortable and I will be embarrassed.*
- *I fear I might become so upset that I'll run out of the restaurant.*

4. Challenge any unhelpful thoughts using the five questions outlined after the exercise 'What feelings are troubling you?' on page 62.

- *It's OK to cry; my friends have been our friends for many years. They are sad too.*
- *It's normal to feel strange going out without Steve at first because it's something new.*
- *In time, I will get used to going on my own.*
- *Steve would want me to go.*

5. Plan how to gradually approach the items you're avoiding, beginning with the easiest.

- *Call my girlfriends and invite them over for a drink or pizza.*
- *Then invite the three couples the following week for a drink.*
- *Plan for the seven of us to go out to a restaurant that we've never been to before.*
- *Finally, plan a night that we can all go to Otto's, our favourite restaurant; make a reservation so I know we definitely have a table.*

6. If needed, break down each item into smaller steps, beginning with the least difficult step. Set a time to try.

By approaching her fears in a systematic way, Janet felt more in control, which allowed her to start building her life without her husband.

Making difficult decisions

There are likely to be many decisions that you will need to make following the death of your loved one, including decisions about financial matters, where to live, sorting through belongings, when to return to work and whether or not to take off your wedding ring. Some choices may be clear to you while others may cause you a great deal of distress. A general rule of thumb is to avoid making major decisions in the first year, especially those that can't be reversed as you're more likely to make a decision based on emotion rather than fact at this time.

Using a framework that you can apply to any decision that you're facing helps make the process easier. The framework outlined below encourages realistic thinking about difficult decisions by focusing on the possible consequences of the different options. If you use this framework you're far less likely to make an impulsive decision that you may regret in the future. As you will see, Pamela used the framework to help her decide whether or not she should sell her husband's vintage car.

Framework for making difficult decisions

Step 1 What is the problem you're experiencing or the decision you're facing?

Whether or not to sell Peter's prized vintage car, which he owned for the last twenty years.

Step 2 How many possible solutions can you list?

Sell or keep.

Step 3 What are the positives and negatives of each of these possible solutions?

Sell: positives: money; negatives: sentimental value, lots of happy memories.

Keep: positives: fond memories, link to Peter; negatives: where to keep it if I move, upkeep, who would drive it? Get less money if I sold it later.

Step 4 Which looks best to you?

Selling is the most sensible option as I really need the money now and can't afford to maintain it.

Step 5 If you used this solution, what would the consequences be?

I would have to deal with the sadness about lost memories and the link to Peter.

Step 6 Can you live with these consequences? Yes/no.

Yes – it would be hard but it's what Peter would recommend as he was always the practical one.

Step 7 If you answered 'No' in Step 6, then go back to Step 2, and work through the remaining steps again.

Step 8 If you use the solution you identified in Step 4 what action do you need to take to try out this solution?

I'd want to take lots of photos before it was sold and maybe have someone take a video. I could ask Peter's friend John to take me on a final drive and make it a special farewell to the old car. Maybe John through the car club would know someone who might like to buy it so that if ever I was really missing it, I could see it again.

Pamela felt much better after thinking about the decision to sell her husband's car in this way. By answering these questions she was able to focus on the consequences of the decision and the steps she would need to take to follow through with her decision. Even though parting with the car would still be very difficult, she was much better prepared. Similarly, the framework can be used when sorting through belongings. It's always best to start with the items that are the least sentimental. If there are things you're not sure about whether to keep or not, keep them for now and revisit your decision in six months' time.

9

Dealing with 'Firsts'

There will be many 'firsts' that you will face within the first year following the death of your loved one. Some of these firsts you will be aware of well in advance and know when they are approaching, such as their birthday or the date they were first diagnosed. Others may take you by surprise. These can include anything from receiving a letter addressed to them to seeing someone who looks just like them. There will also be other firsts in years to come – perhaps a graduation, a wedding or the birth of a grandchild. But typically you mark the majority of firsts in the first twelve months culminating in the first anniversary of your loved one's death. While most people expect that the first anniversary of the death will be hard, many don't realise the impact that all the other firsts can have on them. Being able to face these firsts is an important part of adjusting to your new life.

Look through the following list of firsts. Which ones have you already experienced? Circle the ones that are coming up. What other firsts do you anticipate?

- their birthday

- your birthday

- your wedding anniversary or significant date in your relationship

- the date they were diagnosed

- hearing your special song

- seeing significant friends for the first time

- returning to a special place

- attending a function alone

- Christmas, Hanukkah or other religious holidays

- going on your first holiday alone

- going to the bank

- receiving a letter addressed to your loved one

- watching their favourite sporting team

- seeing a car like theirs.

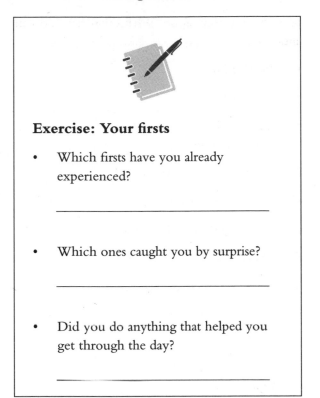

Exercise: Your firsts

- Which firsts have you already experienced?

  _____

- Which ones caught you by surprise?

  _____

- Did you do anything that helped you get through the day?

  _____

Not everyone is affected in the same way when a significant date comes around or when something reminds them of their loved one. But for those who do struggle with firsts, many say that the anticipation of the 'first' is worse than the day itself – which is similar to what people report before they go to the dentist. The best strategy to tackle a first is to make a plan in advance for how you will acknowledge it even if you wish you could skip the date altogether. Making a plan helps because it increases your sense of control.

There are four key components to tackling any first: anticipating the first, planning ahead, developing realistic expectations and reminiscing. The following framework will help you do this.

Framework for tackling firsts

Step 1 *Anticipation* – what firsts are approaching? Where will you be?

Step 2 *Planning* – who do you want to be with? What do you want to do? What arrangements do you need to make ahead of time?

Step 3 *Realistic expectations* – look back over your answers in Step 2. Are these goals realistic? Don't over-commit. Consider lowering your expectations about what you will do this year.

Step 4 *Reminiscing* – what are your favourite memories? Who can you share these with?

Let's look at how Janet planned for the first anniversary of her husband's death.

Janet was dreading the first anniversary. She found herself worrying about her ability to get through the weeks before the anniversary and the actual day itself. By answering the questions above she was able to come up with a plan that she thought would make the day easier to face. It included:

- inviting their special friends and family for a drink on the actual date

- having a guest book for each person to write a fond memory of her husband

- enlarging and framing her favourite photo of her husband to have 'on show'.

What's important to realise is that developing a plan not only gives you a greater sense of control, but also allows you the opportunity to pay attention to your grief. Reminiscing with others or on your own allows you to access fond memories and helps you maintain a connection with the person who has died. Reminiscing helps you acknowledge who they were and what they meant to you. It also gives you opportunities for creating new traditions in their memory, as Janet did.

For those firsts that come out of the blue, there's no time to plan. Instead, it helps if you can check your self-talk soon after the event, reminding yourself that it's OK to feel the way you do, as firsts usually correspond with trigger waves, as we discussed in Part 1. You might find it helpful to tell yourself: 'It's perfectly normal to feel this way because [insert the event] has reminded me of [insert loved one's name] and how much I miss him/her. I know that in time these feelings will ease. This is a normal part of the wave-like pattern of grief.'

Tip

When in doubt about how you will cope with a situation, make a plan.

10

Building Your New Path

People often describe grieving as following a 'two steps forward, one step back' pattern. There is typically a struggle between letting go of their life with their loved one as they knew it and beginning to live a different life without them. It's a struggle that goes back and forth many times. On the one hand you know that you need to build a new life for yourself but on the other hand you don't want to because that means letting go of the life you had before. Eventually, you need to make a conscious decision to build a new or different life to be able to move forward. One important component of making this decision is realising that this doesn't mean forgetting the person or 'getting over' their death. Instead the aim is to find a way to make their memory a part of your life as it is now, which will allow you to maintain a connection with them.

Maintaining a connection

Once the initial shock of the death wears off and your life begins to slowly return to something of what it used to be, it's a good idea to start thinking about how you can develop a new connection with your loved one. This involves working out how you're going to continue to have a connection or relationship with them now they are no longer physically here. This might sound strange, but the aim of dealing with your grief isn't to forget them but to learn to live without them physically in your life. Working out what this new connection looks like – now based on memory and legacy – won't happen immediately. The following questions can help you begin this process.

- Who were they to you?

- What did you learn from them?

- What values did they teach you?

- What did they love about life?

- What history did you share?

- How would they like to be remembered?

- What would you say to them now?

- What is their story?

Often people worry that in time they will forget their loved one. It's true that as time goes on, memories do fade but there are a number of things you can do now to help maintain a connection.

- Tell their story – write a journal about their life.

- Make a memory book – ask friends and family to write something about the person who has died; include different photos from throughout their life.

- Make a DVD compilation of old home videos.

- Make a playlist of their favourite music.

- Visit places that were special to them.

- Donate to or support a cause in their memory.

- Plant a tree.

- Celebrate their birthday.

- Plant their favourite flowers each year.

- Enlarge a special photo and have it framed.

- Continue to share your loved one's jokes, stories and favourite sayings.

- Refer to them by name in conversation.

- Create a new family tradition that keeps them present in your life.

> *Every year I buy a lovely Christmas tree orna-*
> *ment in memory of my daughter who died after a*
> *battle with leukaemia when she was three. I think*
> *about how old she would be and buy something*
> *that seems fitting for a girl that age.*
>
> *Jill, forty-four years*

Your new path

Knowing that you still have a connection with the person who has died makes it easier to decide to work on building your new path. Once you've made this decision, you need to make sure your expectations are realistic about how quickly this will happen. You need to expect some false starts and that the path may be bumpy at times and will take time to build. If you think this way, you won't be shocked when things don't go as smoothly as you thought they would.

The diagram helps explain why building a new path takes time. When we love someone, irrespective of the type of relationship, we have a sense of where our relationship is heading. Unfortunately, with their death, you come to a fork in the path. At the fork you're forced on to another path, one not of your choosing, and you're unsure what lies ahead. The path you were originally on together is no longer an option. Remember that the greatest amount of change and adjustment will probably occur in the initial section of this new path because everything is different. It's important to understand that you're likely to experience lots of ups and downs as you travel along this new path, in much the same way as your grief follows a wave-like pattern with good and bad days, and with trigger waves that come out of the blue. In time this new path will become familiar and feel quite normal as you get used to doing things differently.

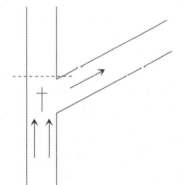

Tips

Keeping your expectations realistic about building your new path

- Expect to have false starts.

- Expect to have ups and downs.

- Expect that your progress may be slow.

- Expect that initially your progress may follow a 'two steps forward, one step back' pattern.

It's a huge challenge to build a new life after the death of someone you love, especially early on, when your grief is raw. Thinking about this too soon can be overwhelming. For this reason, health professionals encourage people who are grieving to take it one day at a time in the beginning, and to avoid making major and potentially irreversible decisions within the first year following the death. Some general guidelines about building a different life for yourself include:

- Create a support system.

- Try new things.

- Ask 'what would my loved one want for me?'

- Set short-term goals.

- Re-examine your identity.

Create a support system

Just as you needed the support of people soon after the death, the same is true when you embark on building your new path. You may already have good support from those who were there in the beginning, but you might also find that your needs change as time goes on and that you need other types of support in addition to this core group. Some people find that they now need to be around people who can encourage them to try different things and who are comfortable with them doing so. It's important to surround yourself with people whose company you enjoy, whom you believe have your best interests at heart, and with whom you feel at ease. If some of your 'supporters' are critical or negative about the changes you're making, you will need to find support elsewhere.

Tips

Creating a support system

- Mix with friends and family with whom you're comfortable.

- Read self-help books or watch self-help DVDs about grief.

- Join a bereavement support group – either locally or online.

- See a grief counsellor.

- Attend a church or religious group.

- Join a group that is specific to your loss. For example, a group for widows/ widowers, for suicide survivors or parents who have lost children.

Try new things

Most people find that their different path involves new things as well as some of the same things that were a part of their old life. You might pursue new interests, while others evolve over time. If you're unsure about where to start, think about the activities or hobbies you've enjoyed in the past.

Tips

Try new things

- Be open to trying new things.

- Seek opportunities to try new things.

- When you attempt to do something for the first time, try it at least twice before you dismiss it as a possibility.

- Be aware of your self-talk. Tell yourself that anything new will feel strange at first.

- Start with whatever is easiest first and gradually build up to doing things that are harder.

- Ask a friend to go with you the first time if you feel a little nervous or awkward about going alone.

- Sometimes, be spontaneous.

- Try things that are inexpensive so that cost doesn't prevent you from continuing.

Exercise: Try new things

- What would you like to do?

- What things have you always wanted to try?

- Are there any organisations you're interested in?

- What would your loved one suggest you try?

- What would be the easiest to try first?

Remember Kate from Part 1? After her husband died she was at a loss to know where to start building her new life. One activity she had always enjoyed was hiking. When Kate completed this exercise, she decided to join a local hiking club with a friend who was divorced. Kate had always enjoyed being outdoors and found it easier to go with her friend than on her own. Kate made new friends and was pleased when she found out the club organised regular trips away to explore other parts of the country, given her desire to travel.

Ask 'what would my loved one want for me?'

In all parts of grief, asking what your loved one would want for you helps you to focus on your future. In relation to building a new path, think about what they would advise if they were sitting next to you now. Most people say that they believe they would want them to be happy. Perhaps you talked about life without each other? What did you discuss? If your roles were reversed, what suggestions would you offer them? As difficult as it might seem, moving forward means trying some new things that may be hard at first to contemplate.

Set short-term goals

Once you start trying new things, you may want to set some goals for what you might like to achieve in the next few months. Start with the short term and make sure your goals are realistic and flexible. Are there things that you would like to do that would give you a sense of purpose?

Exercise: Setting goals

1. What goals would you like to achieve in the next six months? Be specific. Look through the following list to get some ideas.

- Health and fitness

- Hobbies and leisure activities

- Friendships

- Family – children and extended

- Financial planning

- Career or education

- Holidays/vacation

- Community service/volunteer work

_____

_____

2. What action do you need to take to achieve your goals? Be specific and break down each into smaller steps.

_____

_____

As you achieve your goals, continue to set new ones.

Some of Alice's answers (from pages 32–5)

1. Goals:

• *visit Paris*

• *babysit my grandchildren on a regular basis*

2. Action:

• *Do internet research about places to visit; collect brochures from local travel agent about tours; decide on the best time of year and make a reservation.*

• *Talk to Jen about times that would suit her for me to babysit; think about how big a commitment I want*

> to make – probably one day per week; suggest a trial
> run for three months.

By setting goals in this way, Alice was able to travel to Paris and to do some of the things she had planned to do with her husband in their retirement. She also committed to babysitting her grandchildren on a regular basis. Even though her life had not turned out as she had expected, she was still able to find fulfilment and joy.

Re-examine your identity

After the rawness of your grief subsides a little and the majority of the administrative tasks have been finalised, you may find yourself thinking more about your identity and how it has been impacted by the death of your loved one. This is particularly relevant if your spouse or your child has died, as your identity is closely linked to your role within your family and other roles you hold. The best advice is to carve out time to think carefully about re-examining your identity and what it means to you. It is a process that evolves over time and often requires a change in the way you view yourself.

'Bob and I had been married for thirty-eight years. After he died I found myself struggling with the term "widow" as I always had loved being Bob's "wife" and being part of a couple. About eighteen months after his death, I started thinking about who I was now – who Emily was. I knew something needed to change. I started to tell myself that while I would always be Bob's wife, I needed to give myself permission to enjoy my life as a single woman. I don't think I will ever re-marry, but I would like to be able to go out and possibly date – something I know Bob would want me to do.'

Emily, sixty-one years

Exercise: Re-examine your identity

1. How do you define 'identity'?

2. What aspects or components make up who you are? Consider your gender, the different roles you play, your cultural background and so on.

Draw a circle to represent a pie chart. For each aspect that you listed in no. 2, think about how big a piece of the pie each aspect occupies. Draw and label the pieces of your pie.

3.   What happens to your identity when your loved one dies? How does this impact your pie?

4.   What aspects of your life do you want to nurture? Are there new aspects that you would want to add to your pie?

A final word

If you have worked your way through this book, you may still feel as though you have a long way to go. That's perfectly normal. Your challenge now is to continue to work on making your new path the best it can be, even though you wish you were still on your original path. You might find it helpful from time to time to review the strategies and exercises outlined in this book as they might help in different ways at different times. Finally, it's important to have hope as you think about where your life is heading and to remind yourself that moving forward does not mean forgetting your loved one.

Other Things that Might Help

This book has provided you with some basic information about dealing with grief and what may help. Some people will find that this is all they need to feel more able to deal with their loss. Others may need more information or some extra support. Self-help books are a good place to start and some recommendations are listed below. This book is based on *Overcoming Grief*, which will provide you with a more in-depth look at grief and some additional strategies. Alternatively, you may prefer to attend a support group or seek counselling. If you want professional help, consult a therapist, counsellor or psychologist who is experienced in grief counselling.

To find a suitable professional:

- Ask your family doctor to refer you to a qualified counsellor or therapist who deals with grief.

- Contact your national hospice organisation to find a hospice in your area that provides bereavement support.

- Contact your national psychological association for a list of registered psychologists in your area.

- Ask your friends, family or someone from your religious group to recommend a therapist.

We also recommend the following self-help books:

Grieving: How to go on Living when Someone You Love Dies by T. A. Rando, published by Bantam Books (1991)

Helping Bereaved Parents: A Clinician's Guide by R. Tedeschi and L. Calhoun, published by Brunner-Routledge (2004)

Helping Children Cope with Death, published by The Dougy Center for Grieving Children (2004)

No Time for Goodbyes: Coping with Sorrow, Anger and Injustice After a Tragic Death by J. Lord, published by Millennium Books (1987)

Overcoming Grief: A Self-Help Guide Using Cognitive Behavioural Techniques by S. Morris, published by Robinson (2008).

Widow to Widow: Thoughtful, Practical Ideas for Rebuilding your Life by G. D. Ginsburg, published by Da Capo Press (1997)

The following organisations provide information about grief and how to get professional help.

UK

British Association for Counselling and Psychotherapy
Tel: 01455 883300
Email: bacp@bacp.co.uk
Website: www.bacp.co.uk

British Psychological Society
Tel: 0116 254 9568
Email: enquiries@bps.org.uk
Website: www.bps.org.uk

Cruse Bereavement Care
Day by Day Helpline: 0808 808 1677
Email: info@cruse.org.uk and helpline@cruse.org.uk
Website: www.cruse.org.uk

Northern Ireland
Tel: 02890 792419
Email: northern.ireland@cruse.org.uk
Website: www.cruse.org.uk/northern-ireland

Scotland
Tel: 0845 600 2227
Email: info@crusescotland.org.uk
Website: www.crusescotland.org.uk

Samaritans
Free helpline in UK and Ireland
Open 24 hours 116123
www.samaritans.org

USA

Dougy Center for Grieving Children & Families
Toll Free: (866) 775 5683
Email: help@dougy.org
Website: www.dougy.org

National Hospice & Palliative Care Organization
Infoline: 800 658 8898
Email: nhpco_info@nhpco.org
caringinfo@nhpco.org
Website: www.nhpco.org

The Compassionate Friends – Supporting Family After a Child Dies
Toll Free: 877-969-0010
www.compassionatefriends.org

An Introduction to Coping with Insomnia and Sleep Problems

2nd Edition

Colin Espie

ISBN: 978-1-47213-854-5 (paperback)

ISBN: 978-1-47213-892-7 (ebook)

Price: £4.99

Poor sleep can have a huge impact on our health and wellbeing, leaving us feeling run-down, exhausted and stressed out. Written by a leading expert in the field, this simple guide explains the causes of insomnia and why it is so difficult to break bad habits. It gives you clinically proven cognitive behavioural therapy (CBT) techniques for improving the quality of your sleep, showing you how to keep a sleep diary, set personal goals, improve your sleep hygiene, deal with a racing mind and make lasting improvements to your sleeping and waking pattern.

An Introduction to Coping with Phobias

2nd Edition

Brenda Hogan

ISBN: 978-1-47213-852-1 (paperback)

ISBN: 978-1-47213-881-1 (ebook)

Price: £4.99

It's very common for people to have a phobia of something – heights, spiders, water . . . but when that fear prevents you from doing the things you enjoy in life or causes you deep anxiety and feelings of panic, it's time to seek help. This book is a concise, authoritative guide for those whose phobia has become a debilitating problem, and shows you how cognitive behavioural therapy (CBT) can help you overcome your phobia. It encourages you to challenge the way you think and behave, including techniques on how to set your goals, face your fears, problem-solve and avoid relapses.

An Introduction to Coping with Panic

2nd Edition

Charles Young

ISBN: 978-1-47213-853-8 (paperback)
ISBN: 978-1-47213-954-2 (ebook)
Price: £4.99

Panic disorder and panic attacks affect huge numbers of people across the world. This self-help guide explains what panic attacks are, how they develop and what makes them persist. It uses clinically proven cognitive behavioural therapy (CBT) techniques to help you recognise the link between your thoughts and your periods of panic, enabling you to: spot and challenge these thoughts, keep a panic diary and learn calming breathing techniques.

An Introduction to Coping with Health Anxiety

2nd Edition

Brenda Hogan and Charles Young

ISBN: 978-1-47213-851-4 (paperback)

ISBN: 978-1-47213-952-8 (ebook)

Price: £4.99

This book offers guidance for those whose health anxiety or hypochondria have become serious problems and are having a negative impact on their mental health. Through the use of cognitive behavioural therapy (CBT), expert authors Brenda Hogan and Charles Young explain what health anxiety is and how it makes you feel, showing you how to spot and challenge thoughts that make you anxious and reduce your focus on illness. Written in a concise and accessible way, this book gives you both an understanding and an aid for combatting this often-neglected psychological problem.

THE
IMPR⟳VEMENT
ZONE

Looking for life inspiration?

The Improvement Zone has it all, from **expert advice** on how to advance your **career** and boost your **business**, to improving your **relationships**, revitalising your **health** and developing your **mind**.

Whatever your goals, head to our website now.

Swallows

and Spiders

Two stories in One

Julia Donaldson

EGMONT

We bring stories to life

Follow the Swallow was first published in Great Britain 2000
Spinderella was first published in Great Britain 2002
Published in one volume as *Swallows and Spiders* 2012
by Egmont UK Ltd
239 Kensington High Street, London W8 6SA
Text copyright © 2000, 2002 Julia Donaldson
Illustrations copyright © 2000 Martin Ursell; 2002 Liz Pichon
The author and illustrator have asserted their moral rights.
ISBN 978 14052 6209 5
10 9 8 7 6 5 4 3 2 1
A CIP catalogue record for this title is available from the British Library.
Printed in Singapore.